A
Performer's Guide
Through
Historical Keyboard
Tunings

Das I. vnd II. Discant-clavier.

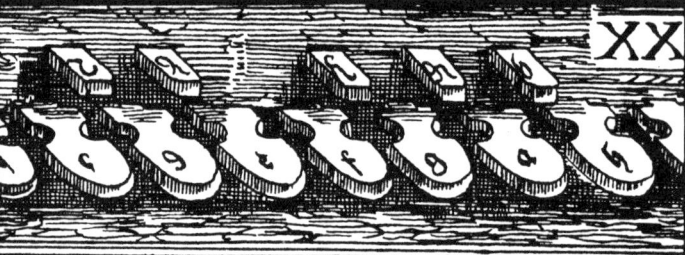

Das III. Clavier.

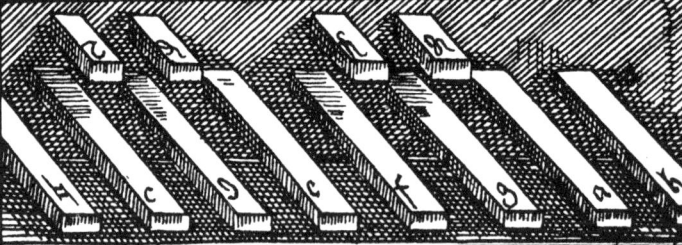

Das IV. Pedal-Clavier.

1361 Halberstadt organ
oldest known fully chromatic keyboard
(woodcut from Praetorius' *Syntagma Musicum* of 1618, 1884 edition)

A Performer's Guide Through Historical Keyboard Tunings
Revised Edition

by
Martin B. Tittle

Anderson Press, Ann Arbor

Copyright © 1978 by Martin B. Tittle

Revised edition copyright © 1987 by Anderson Press

All rights reserved. No part of this book may be reproduced or utilized in any form or by any means without written permission from the publisher. Inquiries should be addressed to: Anderson Press, 706 West Davis, Ann Arbor, Michigan 48103.

Library of Congress Cataloging-in-Publication Data

Tittle, Martin B., 1948-
    A performer's guide through historical keyboard tunings.

    Bibliography: p.
    Includes index.
    1. Keyboard instruments — Tuning. 2. Musical temperament. I. Title.
MT165.T6   1987   786.2'3   87–27095
ISBN 0-942479-01-7 (pbk.)
ISBN 0-942479-02-5 (lib. bdg.)

PRINTED IN THE UNITED STATES OF AMERICA

Table of Contents

Introduction 7
History 9
Tuning: General Considerations 16
Tuning: Specific Temperaments . . . 23
Appendix I: A Parallel Chronology
    of Tuning Genres 39
Appendix II: How to Construct a
    Tuning Recipe 59
Critical Bibliography 70

INTRODUCTION

Tuning, for most of us, is at best uninteresting, and at worst, boring. We have all seen articles and books on this subject before, and have yawned or staggered through their complex mathematics and voluminous historical references without any of it having much effect on our performances.

The question most of these tomes neglect to answer first is, "Why should we care about historical tunings at all?" The reason is that tuning is rightfully a part of performance practice, and so should be just as historically accurate as any other part of our interpretive style. Tuning in keyboard instruments is entirely responsible for the size, and therefore the sound, of all the available intervals, and anyone who has ever heard a pure major third and a Pythagorean one side by side can testify that, while they look the same on the printed page, they are definitely not created equal. Before we ever start playing, the sound of the music we will create has already been predetermined by the tuning, and that's why we should care about it.

The next logical question might be, "Why were these historical tunings ever forgotten if they are really so important to the music?" The truth is, they weren't forgotten at all; they were discarded! The 19th century, with its marvelous technical advances, came to feel that it was somehow the culmination of the past, that the past in most if not all respects had been only an effort toward its own greatness. From this basis, it was obvious that the past must be modernized and its feeble efforts made perfect, so the old instruments, performance practices, and tunings were discarded over a period of years in favor of the piano, Romantic interpretation, and equal temperament. Since then, the pendulum has swung back the other way with the revivals of historically correct instruments, historically accurate interpretation, and finally historical tunings.

Having dispensed with these preliminary considerations, let's outline our approach to this subject. We as performers need to know just enough history to be able to see how different genres of tuning relate to each other and to music, so we'll cover that first. Then we'll deal with general considerations about tuning any temperament, and finally get down to specific tuning recipes for representative examples of the principal types of tunings.

HISTORY

1300 is a good year to begin a history of keyboard tuning because it antedates both the oldest known fully chromatic keyboard (on the 1361 Halberstadt organ) and the oldest music written for such a keyboard (the Robertsbridge Codex, c. 1325-50). The tuning in use around 1300 is today called medieval Pythagorean and is simply a construction of eleven consecutive pure fifths, usually beginning on $G^{\#}$ and descending to E^b.

There are two main features of Pythagorean tuning we need to remember. First, it contains one "wolf," or musically unusable interval, the diminished sixth $G^{\#}$-E^b. Second, it contains two different kinds of major thirds. One is very wide and, consequently, rather harsh-sounding to our ears; the other is, for practical purposes, pure. There are eight of the wide thirds lying in the common keys near C, and four of the near-pure ones in the distant keys of B, $F^{\#}$, $C^{\#}$, and "$G^{\#}$". Of these four, the one on $G^{\#}$ can't be used because it's trapped in the $G^{\#}$-E^b wolf.

The other three, however, form triads that are almost completely pure.

From this information, it's easy to see that medieval Pythagorean had two main attributes: purity, in the form of the 4 pure thirds (and 3 pure triads) in the distant keys, and utility, in the form of 22 usable triads out of the 24 possible in a twelve-note octave. The entire history of Western keyboard tuning from 1300 on is basically the story of various attempts to amplify one of these mutually exclusive attributes at the expense of the other.

The pieces in the Robertsbridge Codex show that the $G^{\#}$-E^b disposition of Pythagorean was still in use when they were written, but as early as the beginning of the 15th century, in the Faenza Codex, we see a transposition of Pythagorean so that the wolf lies elsewhere, usually between B and G^b. This puts the near-pure thirds above D, A, E, and B, where they are used and heard more frequently, and signals that the quest for purity is on. Musicians of this time were fascinated and attracted by the sound of the pure third, and this B-G^b transposition of Pythagorean is documented by Arnaut de Zwolle in the Netherlands, Ugolino of Orvieto in Italy, and many others.

The obvious next step in the search for purity, acoustically, was to try to tune exclusively by pure thirds and pure fifths, a tuning form we call just intonation. Unfortunately, on a keyboard with only twelve notes per octave, just intonation was too limiting to ever get much use. It had only twelve good triads, so composers could only use 50% of the octave's harmonic resources compared to the 90% available in Pythagorean. In addition, it created many wolf intervals which limited harmonic movement unbearably. Since the emphasis in the search for purity was on pure major thirds, a collective decision was made in the mid-1400's to temper, or intentionally damage the purity of the fifths, in favor of getting more useful triads.

This type of tuning, with the narrow fifths and relatively pure thirds, is called meantone, and for a tuning system based on the pure major third, it is the ultimate. If we insist on both pure thirds and pure octaves, only two of the three consecutive major thirds that comprise each octave can ever be pure at any one time. The remaining third will really be a diminished fourth, which sounds badly out of tune and is almost worthless as a musical interval. Thus, meantone allows use of two-thirds of the octave's harmonic resources, or 16 out of the 24 possible triads, and while this may sound like a rather puny addition to just intonation's resources, it was significant, as evidenced by the large body of 16th- and 17th-century works written for meantone.

The Buxheim Organ Book, compiled around 1470, shows the transition from transposed Pythagorean to meantone beautifully: its settings of 15th-century songs display the B–G^b Pythagorean orientation, while its original pieces clearly show a meantone temperament in use.

Flow Chart for
HISTORY OF KEYBOARD TUNING
1300 – 1850

1300
PYTHAGOREAN
all fifths pure
only one "wolf" – $G^\#$-E^b
2 types M3rds – pure & very wide
22 usable triads

|

"search for purity"

|

early 1400's
TRANSPOSED PYTHAGOREAN
pure M3rds in common keys

|

late 1400's
MEANTONE
pure M3rds & narrow 5ths
16 usable triads
several wolves
no enharmonicity

"search for
utility"

1691
WELL TEMPERAMENT
narrow meantone 5ths
&
pure Pythagorean 5ths
complete enharmonicity
no wolves
M3rds vary, pure to very wide
"key colors"

1800-1850
EQUAL TEMPERAMENT
all 5ths slightly, equally narrow
all like intervals (M3, m3, etc.) same size
no key colors
complete enharmonicity

In addition to the limitation on harmonic resources, meantone imposed another restriction on composers: it allowed no enharmonicity. Today, with our heritage of 135 years of equal temperament, we almost take enharmonicity for granted, but meantone allows no such familiarity. If the raised key between G and A is tuned pure to E, then it is a $G^\#$ and nothing else. Play it with C, and we'll have just what the printed page says: a diminished fourth, which sounds literally awful. So where Pythagorean had only one wolf, the unusable $G^\#$-E^b, meantone has several.

Although meantone continued in use through the mid-19th century, the mainstream of music had taken several different turns by then. Around the end of the 17th century, composers began to need and want enharmonicity, a problem they had been rather ingeniously avoiding for some time, and this signals a shift from the search for purity to the search for utility.

In 1691, the German theoretician Werckmeister described a type of tuning called *wohl temperiert* which used both the narrow fifths of meantone and the pure fifths of Pythagorean. This "well temperament" provided complete enharmonicity, eliminated all the wolves present in previous tuning systems, and made all tonalities available for use. The important feature that distinguished it from equal temperament, which also offered these advantages, was its creation of color effects for the different keys. Well temperament had several different sizes of major thirds, varying from the pure thirds of meantone to the wide thirds of Pythagorean, and they were arranged so as to change size gradually around the circle of fifths. Those thirds closest to C were the most pure and tranquil, while those furthest from C were the widest and most dissonant.

This coloristic effect of the different keys had two uses: modulatory contrast, so the listener was given a real aural change when the tonic shifted, and augmentation of a work's character. This latter use can be easily demonstrated on a well-tempered instrument by transposing the first prelude from Book I of the *Well-Tempered Clavier* to $C^\#$, and then playing it properly in C. $C^\#$, with its wide third, has a bubbly vivacity which is clearly inappropriate for the tranquil arpeggiations of this prelude, while the much purer third of C accentuates its calm, stately progressions. $C^\#$ is perfect for the third prelude, with its lively oscillating 16th notes, and when this prelude is transposed to C, it sounds dull and muted. Thus, well temperament not only provided needed enharmonicity, it added a coloristic dimension to music which gave the doctrine of the affections a real vehicle for expression.

Around the turn of the 19th century, however, music became more densely textured and much more harmonically complex, to the extent that these key colors began to get in the way, and this led to the rise of equal temperament, the tuning we use today. Equal temperament had complete enharmonicity, but differed from well temperament in having only one size fifth and one size major third. This allowed all triads and tonalities to have the same color, so composers could modulate from one to another without a jangle of colors to interrupt their transition. Equal temperament had always had its adherents in earlier centuries, but only now did the needs of the majority of composers allow it to become dominant.

And that is all we as performers need to know about the history of keyboard tuning. If we can visualize in one mental picture the progression through five centuries from medieval Pythagorean to the purity of meantone, on to the partial purity and increased utility of well temperaments, and finally on to the total impurity and increased versatility of equal temperament, then we understand the performing aspects of this subject. For the curious who want more detailed information, a parallel chronology of the persons, events, and documents which chronicle these four tuning genres is included as Appendix I.

TUNING:
GENERAL CONSIDERATIONS

In keyboard tuning, we have to tune both tempered and pure intervals. To tune the former, we need an understanding of the phenomenon of "beats" and how to use them in common tempered intervals. To tune pure intervals we need to know the checks that prove and insure their absolute purity. Before discussing either of these matters, however, it might be best to get a few fundamentals out of the way.

First of all, when we decide to tune a certain note, it's best to start by dropping the pitch slightly regardless of where we eventually want to move it. That way, if we're not on the right pin, we'll find out without the danger of breaking a string.

Next, we should continually remind ourselves not to succumb to the temptation to bend the tuning pins when the pitch is almost correct and needs only a small adjustment. Tuning pins should be turned, and bending just distorts the pin, crushes the pinblock, and creates an unstable tuning in the process.

Third, if we are going to temper an interval, we should remember to tune it pure first and then make it wide or narrow as the tuning directions instruct. Trying to shoot straight for the end result without this intermediate step many times gives us an interval which beats correctly but is entirely wrong because it's tempered on the incorrect side of pure.

Fourth, we should never try to do a really nice tuning if the pitch of the instrument has to be changed any appreciable amount. Better to go through all the registers two or even three times than to struggle for the impossible goal of stability and accuracy while the soundboard is heaving under the stress of large tensile changes.

Finally, if we think we have a false string, we should check to make sure it is firmly seated on the nut and bridge. A string which has climbed its pin at either of these locations will sound false even if the wire itself is perfect.

Now let's talk about beats. Why? Because they're the basis for and major tool of aural tuning. For performing musicians, beats might be best described as a "wah-wah" sound caused by the partials or overtones of two notes being out of tune with each other. With an out-of-tune unison, which we've all heard, all the partials of the two strings are out of tune with each other. With most tempered intervals, however, only two partials, one from each of the two strings, lie close enough to the same frequency to beat. So the key, or secret in hearing the beats in tempered intervals is knowing the frequency at which the beating is taking place. If we then focus our attention on that frequency, the beat, which may have been inaudible before, usually becomes clear as day. There is a complicated way for figuring out this beating frequency for any interval, but it's probably simpler if we just state how to find it for the common intervals we have to temper in most tunings. The chart in Figure 1 (p. 20) provides this information in a tabular format that is easier to understand and use than the equivalent prose would be.

Now let's get down the checks for pure intervals. We will probably be tuning only four different pure intervals: octaves, fourths, fifths, and major thirds, and the checks for the first three of these are especially useful since we commonly have to tune them in series, where the ultimate accuracy of each succeeding interval depends on the purity of all those that came before it.

To prove that a fourth is really pure, use the note a major third below its lower note and a major sixth below its upper note (see Figure 2a). This configuration can be viewed as the first inversion of a minor triad if it helps us visualize it better. The major third and the major sixth should beat the same, regardless of what that beat is and regardless of whether the note we've interpolated below the fourth has been tuned yet or not. In our example, the fourth is e-a, so we interpolate c below it and check to make sure the major third c-e beats the same as the major sixth c-a. (The diamond-shaped notes on the small treble staff above the example just show the position of the beating partials, to remind us where to listen.)

The proof for a pure major third uses this same first inversion minor triad configuration, except that we listen to see if the major sixth and perfect fourth beat the same. In the example (Figure 2b), c-e is pure because c-a and e-a beat the same at the e^2 partial level.

To prove that a fifth is pure, we make it into a minor triad in root position by adding the appropriate note in the middle, and then check to see that the two thirds in the minor triad beat the same. In the

Figure 1

BEAT LOCATIONS FOR COMMON TEMPERED INTERVALS

If the interval is:
- C-E (major third),
- C-E^b (minor third),
- C-G (perfect fifth),
- C-F (perfect fourth),
- C-A (major sixth),

THEN

we should listen for the beat at:
- e^1 (2 8ves + M3 ↑ from C).
- g^1 (2 8ves + P5 ↑ from C).
- g (1 8ve + P5 ↑ from C).
- c^1 (2 8ves ↑ from C).
- e^1 (2 8ves + M3 ↑ from C).

Figure 2

CHECKS FOR PURE INTERVALS

A. Fourths

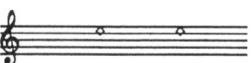

Pure Fourth   M3 - M6 Check

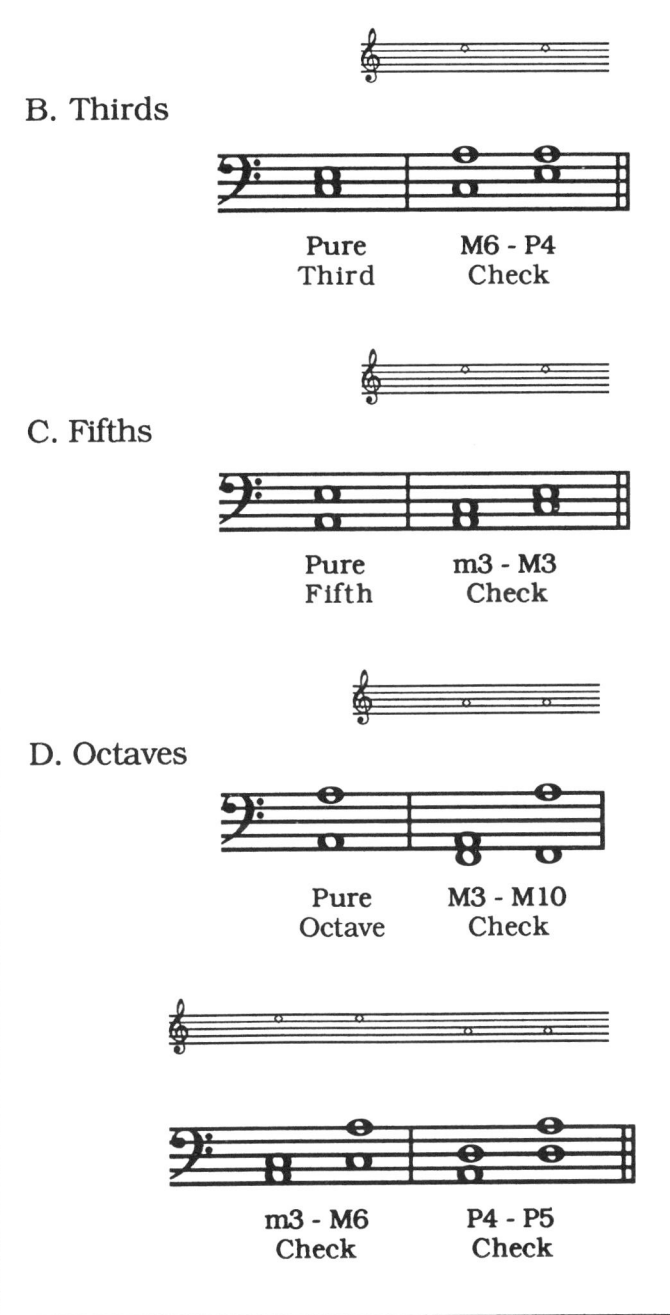

example, our fifth is A-e, so we add c in the middle and insure that A-c beats the same as c-e. Again, it doesn't matter whether c has been tuned yet or not, as long as it's definitely some sort of c and not a $B^\#$ or c^b.

There are three checks for pure octaves, so we can choose whichever is easiest, or use different ones in different areas of the keyboard. As Figure 2d shows, the first check just adds a major third below the octave and requires the resulting major third and major tenth to beat the same. With the octave A-a, we'd add F and see if F-A beats equally with F-a. This check can even be expanded for checking double octaves, in which case the major seventeenth formed by F and a^1 would still beat the same as the other two check intervals.

The other two octave checks operate by dividing the octave rather than adding a note outside it. One divides the octave into a lower minor third and an upper major sixth, saying, again, that both intervals beat the same when the octave is pure. Example: A-a is pure when A-c beats the same as c-a. The other check divides the octave into a lower fourth and an upper fifth which beat equally. Example: A-a is pure when A-d beats the same as d-a.

In closing the general comments on tuning, let's not forget the relative importance of the various areas of tuning. The most important tuning we do in preparing our instruments is tuning the two 8' registers in unison, because unison errors are the easiest to hear and are perhaps the most offensive. Next in importance will be the octaves, both within each register and between the 4' and 8' strings, since errors here will again protrude mercilessly in our performance. Least in importance, contrary to popular thought, is the temperament, so if we can't temper perfectly, we shouldn't think all is lost. Rather, we should just do the best we can and then get those unisons and octaves perfect. Unless our tempering error is really bad, this will get us by while we improve tempering through practice. Similarly, if we have only a short time to tune, we should adopt a "get-it-right-but-get-it-quick" attitude toward the temperament and spend the majority of time on the octaves and unisons.

In tuning fortepianos, one further step will increase tuning stability, and that is to strike each note one or two good, fortissimo blows before going to the next. This sends a sharp shock wave down the strings, equalizing the tension of the strings between the various friction points at the nut and bridge, and should be done every time a string is tuned or retuned.

TUNING:
SPECIFIC TEMPERAMENTS

For schematic diagrams of five of the six tuning recipes we will discuss, see Figure 3. In these diagrams, the white notes are the ones being tuned in each

Figure 3a

MEANTONE
1/4-comma — "Praetorius"

𝅗𝅥 = note being tuned   𝅘𝅥 = note already tuned

M.M.   98   131   87
Beats/Sec.   -0-   1.6   2.2   1.5   -0-   -0-

(Pure with Tuning Fork)

M.M.
Beats/Sec.   -0-   -0-   -0-   -0-   -0-   -0-

M.M.
Beats/Sec.   -0-   -0-   -0-   -0-   -0-

(Alternate Accidentals)

25

Figure 3b

MEANTONE
— 1/6-comma — "Silbermann"

♩ = note being tuned   ♩ = note already tuned

M.M.		66	84	60	197	244
Beats/Sec.	-0-	1.1	1.4	1.0	3.3	4.1

(Pure with Tuning Fork)

M.M.	295	364	217	273	326	
Beats/Sec.	4.9	6.1	3.6	4.6	5.4	-0-

M.M.	204	176	229	231	263	306
Beats/Sec.	3.4	2.9	3.8	3.8	4.4	5.1

(Alternate Accidentals)

WELL TEMPERAMENT
1/4-comma — "Werckmeister"

♩ = note being tuned   ♩ = note already tuned

M.M.
Beats/Sec. -0- -0- -0- -0- -0- -0-

(Pure with Tuning Fork)

M.M.   159   119   178
Beats/Sec. -0-   2.6   2.0   3.0   -0-   -0-

M.M.   150
Beats/Sec.   2.5

(Resultant)

Figure 3d

WELL TEMPERAMENT
1/6-comma — "Vallotti"

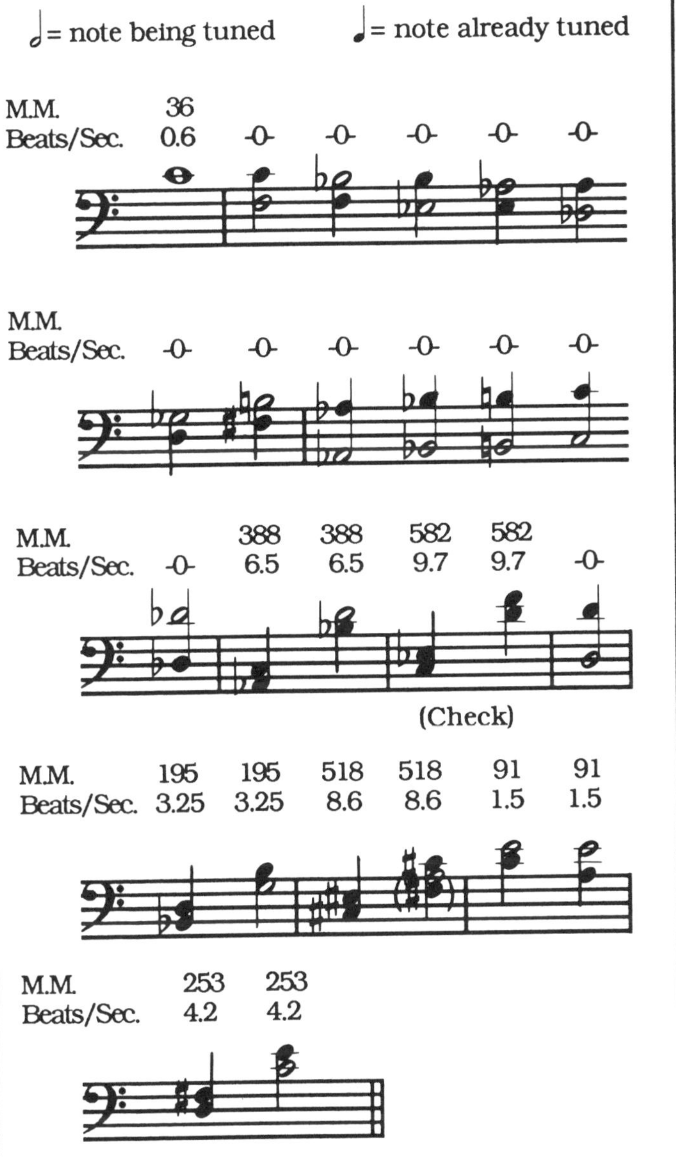

♩ = note being tuned　　♩ = note already tuned

28

Figure 3e

EQUAL TEMPERAMENT SUBSTITUTE
1/3-comma – "Marpurg"

𝅗𝅥 = note being tuned   𝅘𝅥 = note already tuned

M.M.   179
Beats/Sec.   -0-   -0-   -0-   -0-   3.0   -0-

(Pure with
Tuning Fork)

M.M.   113   142
Beats/Sec. -0-   -0-   1.9   -0-   -0-   -0-   2.4

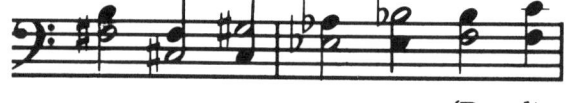

(Resultant)

M.M.   190   239   301   159   201   253
Beats/Sec.   3.2   4.0   5.0   2.7   3.3   4.2

Transposition I   Transposition II

M.M.   168   212   267
Beats/Sec.   2.8   3.5   4.5

Transposition III

interval, and the black notes, the ones that have already been tuned. Bar lines divide the procedures into "measures" at appropriate points. Above each interval are two numbers. The lower is the beat speed of the interval in beats per second, the common way of stating how tempered an interval is to be. The number on top is a metronome marking, in case this is more helpful in feeling how fast the beats will be. Using it may sometimes give a better idea of the beating involved, since the beats-per-second figure is rounded to the nearest 1/10 of a beat, while the metronome marking is figured using the original exact beat speed computation. All these beat speed figures have been computed at modern pitch (A=440 Hz.), but if we want to tune and play at low pitch (A=415 Hz., one equal—tempered half step below A-440), there's an easy and accurate way to convert them: divide each by 1.0594631. With a pocket calculator, this just takes a few seconds per tuning since, after the first conversion, we have only to key in the beat speed and hit "=".

Regardless of pitch level, the metronome markings are sometimes above the metronome scale, so we have to do some logical interpolation. For instance, if the metronome marking given is 436, that could easily be 16th notes at 109 or triplets at 145.

In all cases shown here, fifths and minor thirds are to be tempered narrower than pure, and fourths and major thirds, wider than pure.

The word *comma* preceded by a fraction occurs in the name of all the tuning recipes and refers to the mathematics involved in the construction of each tuning. It's not defined or explained because we as performers don't need to know the nuts and bolts of tuning design to choose appropriate tunings for our performances and execute them properly on our instruments. For the curious or theoretically minded among us who want to get involved in this behind-the-scenes aspect of tuning, Appendix II, "How to Construct a Tuning Recipe," will be required reading. Now, on to tunings.

There is no schematic diagram for medieval Pythagorean, because it's too simple to require one and we rarely if ever need it for performance. If we wish to tune it, just begin with middle C, tune through the flats to E^b by pure fifths and fourths, and then go back to C and tune through the sharps to $G^{\#}$ the same way, checking the purity of each fifth and fourth along the way. The major thirds above B, $F^{\#}$, $C^{\#}$, and $G^{\#}$ will come out almost pure if our line of fifths and fourths is accurate, and the other thirds will have that shrill, uncountable beat speed which justified their being called "imperfect consonances" at best and dissonances at worst. For the $B\text{-}G^b$ transposition of Pythagorean, just stop at E-B when tuning through the sharps and extend the fifths and fourths on the flat side past E^b to A^b, D^b, and finally G^b. As we noted earlier, this will cause the pure major thirds to lie above D, A, E, and B.

The first tuning schematic is for the most common variety of meantone tuning, 1/4-comma meantone. Notice that even though every fifth in this tuning is tempered, this tuning recipe only requires us to temper three directly; the others all turn out correctly tempered when we lay in the pure major thirds. First, after tuning middle C pure to our tuning fork, we tune the fifth F-C so it beats slightly more than 1 1/2 beats per second (M.M. 98). Then the fourth F-B^b is set wide at a fast 2 beats per second (M.M. 131). Next, E^b-B^b is narrowed to exactly 1 1/2 beats per second (M.M. 87), and compared with the F-C to make sure it's slightly slower. From there on, we add all the other notes by tuning them as pure thirds from these four. From C, tune pure up to E, and then pure up to G$^\#$ from E. From F, get A and C$^\#$. From B^b, get D and F$^\#$. Finally, from E^b, derive G and B. If our music calls for accidentals other than these (F$^\#$, C$^\#$, B^b, E^b, and G$^\#$), we go back and retune the appropriate raised keys. For G^b, tune a pure third with B^b; for D^b, a pure third with F. A$^\#$ is a pure third above F$^\#$, D$^\#$ a pure third above B, and A^b a pure third below C.

Another important variety of meantone is 1/6-comma meantone (see Figure 3b). It was attributed to Silbermann by Sorge and, in contrast to 1/4-comma, its major thirds are not pure but slightly widened. In the tuning recipe we begin again with the same three intervals, C-F, F-B^b, and B^b-E^b, but this time we slow the beats down in each.

In beginning, listen carefully to the difference between 60 (1 beat per second) and 66 (1.1 beats per second) on the metronome. Then set F a pure fifth below C and raise it until the beats match M.M. 66. Next set B^b pure above F and raise it until it matches M.M. 84. Finally, lay in E^b below B^b so its beats match M.M. 60.

Now we're ready to tune the major thirds and see how the care we took with these first three intervals pays off. Tune G above E^b and make the beats run 3 times as fast as the beating in F-C. (Hear the F-C beats as quarter notes and the E^b-G beats as triplet eighths.) Next tune B a major third above G and make it beat roughly 4 times as fast as E^b-B^b. Then lay in D above B^b and $F^\#$ above D, and make these thirds beat about 5 and 6 times as fast as E^b-B^b respectively. With this done, we can now slip the remaining 4 major thirds into place between these correctly tempered thirds and rough set their beat rates. Drop in F-A between E^b-G and G-B by tuning A slightly sharp of pure until the beat rate of F-A is intermediate to those of its neighbors. Then do the same with A-$C^\#$ and C-E. E-$G^\#$, the final third, could be set "freehand" above C-E at 6.8 b.p.s. (M.M. 408), but it's easier to go back down and drop it in between E^b-G and F-A, making it beat faster than E^b-G and yet slower than F-A. As before, alternate accidentals may be substituted for the normal compass of chromatics if required by the music.

For well temperament we have two representative samples. The first is by

Werckmeister (see Figure 3c) and is the one he himself favored most out of the many he devised. Begin with C as usual and tune pure fifths and fourths through the flats to G^b. Then go back to C and set G, D, and A as the schematic shows. (That the beat rate of G-C at 2.6 b.p.s. falls almost exactly between the 2 b.p.s. of G-D and the 3 b.p.s. of A-D is just serendipity.) From A tune a pure fifth up to E, and then a pure fourth back down to B. The $F^\#$-B resultant fourth should beat no faster than the G-C fourth, and ideally a hair slower. If it doesn't, and all our pure intervals are accurate and clean, we probably made an error in the C-G-D-A sequence. Using a watch with a sweep second hand, count the beats in each of the three intervals over a period of 5 seconds. G-C should yield 13 solid beats in 5 seconds, G-D should yield 10, and A-D, 15. Listening at the proper pitch level — even playing that pitch softly before sounding the interval — will make beats easier to hear.

The second well temperament, labelled "1/6-comma — 'Vallotti'," was practiced in Padua by organist and composer Francesco Antonio Vallotti from 1730-80 and was reportedly praised by Tartini for the shading and variety it allowed (see Figure 3d). This temperament was rediscovered in 1970 by van Biezen and in 1982 by Fairchild, and is very similar to Thomas Young's Temperament No. 2 of 1800. Of our two well temperaments, the Vallotti will probably be better for late 18th-century compositions, and the Werckmeister, for early 18th-century works.

This tuning recipe will be somewhat different than the others we've tuned thus far in that it will involve setting middle C once in the beginning, and then retuning it differently at the end. The benefit of this extra work is a much easier and more accurate tuning scheme. Begin by tuning C, not exactly to the tuning fork, but 0.6 b.p.s., or 3 beats in 5 seconds, higher. Then tune a series of pure fifths and fourths through the flats to C^b. (Since there is complete enharmonicity in well temperaments, we can redesignate G^b-C^b, $F^\#$-B before proceeding.) Next tune and check carefully lower octaves off A^b, B^b, B, and C, and an upper octave off D^b/$C^\#$. Now we are ready to temper D, G, A, E, and finally C, in that order. Set D above B^b so that the B^b-D major third beats exactly the same as the A^b-C major third an octave lower. As a check after setting D, play C-E^b in the bass and D-F above middle C: they should beat exactly the same, too. Then tune and check carefully a lower octave off this freshly tuned D. Next lay in G below B and make the G-B third beat the same as B^b-D below it. Then tune A below $C^\#$ so it beats the same as $C^\#$-$E^\#$. Since the $F^\#$-$C^\#$ fifth is pure (we tuned it as the fourth D^b-G^b), the minor third $F^\#$-A should also beat the same as $C^\#$-$E^\#$. Next comes E, laid in above C so that the third C-E beats the same as the fifth A-E. Finally we retune the C-E third we just set, adjusting the C downward so that C-E beats the same as D-$F^\#$.

Since this is the only equal–beating

tuning scheme we will use, it deserves some comment and explanation. Very seldom in the conversion of a tuning from its theoretical statement in commas and cents to a practical statement in Herz and beats per second do we find equal-beating intervals that are useful in tuning. We know that the intervals we use to check pure fifths, fourths, and thirds beat the same, but they could beat the same at 3 b.p.s., 6 b.p.s., or any other level. Equal-beating intervals used to set a tuning must beat equally at one spot, and one spot only, and the natural occurence of such phenomena is rare. Most equal-beating tuning recipes, therefore, contain distortions, or changes in the beat speeds of certain intervals so that they arbitrarily match others. For instance, in Owen Jorgensen's equal-beating recipe for setting the Werckmeister we just tuned, he says to set D between B^b and $F^\#$ so that B^b-D and D-$F^\#$ beat equally. Setting the D just above middle C thusly creates a beat rate of about 7.3 b.p.s. for each of these two thirds. The actual beat rates which the Werckmeister scheme creates for these intervals, however, would be 6.5 b.p.s. for B^b-D and 8.2 b.p.s. for D-$F^\#$. In creating the Vallotti recipe above similar but smaller changes were made. The beat rates of various major thirds in the Vallotti were altered by as much as 3/10 b.p.s. from their theoretical ideals to create the equal-beating recipe presented.

For the final tuning in our catalog of recipes it would seem logical to arrive at equal temperament, but instead, on our schematic diagrams, we see an "equal temperament substitute" labelled "1/3-comma — 'Marpurg'." There's no evidence this tuning was ever used, but it does create major thirds exactly the same as those of equal temperament. At the same time, it's much easier to tune, requiring only two tempering steps instead of equal temperament's eleven, so for our purposes, it's a reasonable acoustic substitute. The Marpurg contains three tempered fifths spaced equidistantly by major thirds, and it is this equidistant spacing that allows it to be transposed without being substantially changed. Thus we may choose the disposition of tempered fifths, or conversely the position of the pure fifths, which best suits our musical needs.

Begin by tuning C to the tuning fork and proceed through pure fifths and fourths to A. Now set E a pure fourth below A and then lower it until E-A beats 3 times per second (M.M. 179). Continue from E with pure fifths and fourths through the sharps to $G^\#$, and then lower $G^\#$ until $C^\#$-$G^\#$ beats 1.9 b.p.s. (M.M. 113). Then make the mental transition from $G^\#$ to A^b, and continue with pure fourths and fifths through the flats to F. The F-C fifth which is never tuned but which results from the first and last notes of this recipe should beat 2.4 times per second (M.M. 142).

Now we have the Marpurg in its original, untransposed position, with tempered fifths between A-E, $C^\#$-$G^\#$, and F-C. The first transposed position moves these three fifths up a half step to B^b-F, D-A, and $F^\#$-$C^\#$. The second transposed position pulls them up further to B-$F^\#$, E^b-B^b, and G-D, and the third transposed position completes the cycle by placing them at C-G, E-B, and A^b-E^b. For these three transposed positions, the tuning recipe provides only the beat speeds of the tempered intervals, leaving us as tuner/performers to find our own way to them using the directions for the original position as a pattern. If, in so doing, it is desirable to invert any of the fourths provided so they can be tuned as fifths, the appropriate beat speeds should be halved. For instance, if F-B^b in the first transposed position were inverted by dropping the B^b one octave, the beat speed for the B^b-F fifth would be one half of 3.2, or 1.6 b.p.s. If, on the other hand, the F were moved up an octave to create a B^b-F fifth bridging middle C, the beat speed would be unaltered. (This latter case should sound at least a bit familiar: it's the fourth-fifth check for pure octaves.) When the tuning is finished, go through and play a chromatic scale in major thirds, listening to the beats produced by each one. They should get gradually faster from one to the next, so if there's a jump between two adjacent thirds, or two that beat the same, that error will have to be cleaned up before we expand the temperament to the rest of the instrument.

APPENDIX I

A PARALLEL CHRONOLOGY

OF TUNING GENRES

The following chronology lists a variety of historia that relate to keyboard tuning: composers, compositions, instruments, events, authors, and so on. Hopefully, if we have a question about a certain year or decade, or want to place a name or event in perspective, it will be helpful. I've given up trying to make it complete or objective. I add to it regularly, but the decisions of what to include and what to pass by are, I'm afraid, hopelessly personal. A few abbreviations are used throughout: the punctuation mark "," for the word *comma*, as in "1/4,"; and "M3○" for "pure major third," "P5−" for "narrowed perfect fifth," and so on.

A PARALLEL CHRONOLOGY

PYTHAGOREAN TUNING	MEANTONE "Praetorius' Temperament"
c. 540 B.C. - Pythagoras of Samos	
1340 - Robertsbridge Codex (c. 1325-1350) - shows full chromatic keyboard; G#-Eb disposition	
1361 - Halberstadt organ - first documented fully chromatic keyboard	
early 1400's - Faenza Codex - uses B-Gb or perhaps F#-Db disposition	
1430 - Ugolino (1380-1457) - B-Gb disposition	
1434 - Anselmi (c. 1386-1440) - Bb-Gbb disposition; influenced Gaffurius	

OF TUNING GENRES

WELL TEMPERAMENT	EQUAL TEMPERAMENT "Rameau's Temperament"
	c. 400 - Ho Tcheng-Tien (c.370-447)
1373 - English organ with chromatics set as meantones	

A PARALLEL CHRONOLOGY

PYTHAGOREAN TUNING	MEANTONE "Praetorius' Temperament"
1440 - Arnaut (c. 1400-1466) - B - G^b disposition	
c. 1470 - Buxheim Organ Book — song settings use B-G^b disposition	c. 1470 - Buxheim Organ Book - original pieces, including *Fundamentum* of Paumann (1410-1473)
	1480 - cathedral organ, Lucca
1482 - Ramos (c. 1440-1491) - G - E^{bb} disposition	1482 - Ramos (c. 1440-1491)
1492 - Gaffurius (1451-1522) - B - G^b disposition	
	1511 - Schlick (1460-1521) - M3+
	1520 - Gaffurius (1451-1522)

OF TUNING GENRES

WELL TEMPERAMENT	EQUAL TEMPERAMENT "Rameau's Temperament"
1496 - Gaffurius (1451-1522) - ?	
1511 - Schlick (1460-1521) - ?	
1518 - Grammateus (1492-1525) - 1/2, (B♭-F, B-F♯)	

A PARALLEL CHRONOLOGY

PYTHAGOREAN TUNING	MEANTONE "Praetorius' Temperament"
	1521 - Spataro (1458-1541)
	1523 - Aron (1480-1550)
	1530 - Salinas (1513-1590) - 1/4,
	1533 - Lanfranco (1490-1545) - M3+
	1558 - Zarlino (1517-1590) - 2/7, M3–
	1565 - Tomás de Santa María (d. 1580)
	1571 - Zarlino (1517-1590) - 1/3, less sonorous than 1/4, ("new") and 2/7,
	1577 - Salinas (1513-1590) - 1/3, m3 ○
1596 - Stevin uses Pythag. as theoretical ideal in calculating = temperament	

OF TUNING GENRES

WELL TEMPERAMENT	EQUAL TEMPERAMENT "Rameau's Temperament"
	1530 - Willaert (1490-1562)
	1567 - Orso
	1577 - Salinas (1513-1590)
	1588 - Zarlino (1517-1590)
	1596 - Chu Tsai-Yu
	1596 - Simon Stevin (1548-1620)

A PARALLEL CHRONOLOGY

PYTHAGOREAN TUNING	MEANTONE "Praetorius' Temperament"
1600 - present - Pythag. still in day-to-day use in provincial areas	1600 - Verheyen - letter to Stevin - 1/3, 2/7, 1/4, 1/5,
	1618 - Praetorius (c.1569-1621) -1/4,
	1627 - Mersenne (1588-1648) - *Traité de l'harmonie universelle* - 1/3, 1/4, 2/7,
	1635 - Mersenne - *Harmonicorum libri*
	1637 - Mersenne - *Harmonie Universelle* - 1/4,

OF TUNING GENRES

WELL TEMPERAMENT	EQUAL TEMPERAMENT "Rameau's Temperament"
	1626 - Gallé teaches Severin to make transposing keyboards for = temp.
1635 - Mersenne misinterpreted	1635 - Mersenne (1588-1648) - *Harmonicorum libri*
	late 1630's - Frescobaldi (1583-1643) via "an old Sicilian"
	late 1630's - Froberger (1616-1667)

A PARALLEL CHRONOLOGY

PYTHAGOREAN TUNING	MEANTONE "Praetorius' Temperament"
1600 - present - Pythag. still in day-to-day use in provincial areas	
	1643 - Denis (c. 1600-1672) - P5– "un poinct"; M3 "good"
	early 1700's - Silbermann (1683-1753) - 1/6,
	1700's - English keyboard tutors incl. Pasquali (1718-1757) - 1/5,?

OF TUNING GENRES

WELL TEMPERAMENT	EQUAL TEMPERAMENT "Rameau's Temperament"
	1640 - unnamed mathematician (possibly Gallé) advocates = temp. in Paris; Denis dismayed
	1680-1720 - German theorists: Neidhardt, Werckmeister, etc.
	1688 - first organ tuned to = temperament in Hamburg
1691 - Werckmeister (1645-1706)	
1700 - Croft (1678-1727)	

A PARALLEL CHRONOLOGY

PYTHAGOREAN TUNING	MEANTONE "Praetorius' Temperament"
1600 - present - Pythag. still in day-to-day use in provincial areas	(1700's - Eng. keyboard tutors including Pasquali (1718 - 1757) - 1/5, ?)
	1726 - North (1651-1734) - M3+
	1748 - Smith (1689-1768)

OF TUNING GENRES

WELL TEMPERAMENT	EQUAL TEMPERAMENT "Rameau's Temperament"
1722 - WTC, Part I, Cöthen	
1724 - Neidhardt (1685-1739)	1724 - Neidhardt specifies = temp. as temp. for court
1726 - Rameau (1683-1764)	
1730 - Vallotti (1697-1780)	
	1737 - Rameau recants 1726 advocacy of well temp. & endorses = temp.
1739 - Mattheson (1681-1764) - friend of Handel; hails doctrine of the affections	
1744 - WTC, Part II, Leipzig	
1748 - Rousseau (1712-1778) - ident. keys by ear	1748 - Sorge (1703-1778)
	1753 - C. P. E. Bach (1714-1788)

A PARALLEL CHRONOLOGY

PYTHAGOREAN TUNING	MEANTONE "Praetorius' Temperament"
1600 - present - Pythag. still in day-to-day use in provincial areas	(1700's - Eng. keyboard tutors including Pasquali (1718 - 1757) - 1/5, ?)

OF TUNING GENRES

WELL TEMPERAMENT	EQUAL TEMPERAMENT "Rameau's Temperament"
	1756 - Fritz (1697-1766)- "Schubert tuning"
	1756 - Marpurg (1718-1795)
	1760 - Kirnberger (1721-1783)
	1770 - Heck (1740?-1791?)
1775 - Handel (1685 - 1759) - tuning pub. in *Voluntaries IV*; authenticity doubted	
1776 - Kirnberger (1721-1783) - student of J. S. Bach; reports JSB tuned M3+; friend of Quantz, CPEB, & Marpurg	
1776 - Marpurg (1718 - 1795) - friend of Kirnberger and Forkel	1776 - Marpurg again
	1782 - Bossler (d. 1812)

A PARALLEL CHRONOLOGY

PYTHAGOREAN TUNING	MEANTONE "Praetorius' Temperament"
1600 - present - Pythag. still in day-to-day use in provincial areas	(1700's - Eng. keyboard tutors including Pasquali (1718 1757) - 1/5, ?)
	1806 - Hawkes - 1/5,

OF TUNING GENRES

WELL TEMPERAMENT	EQUAL TEMPERAMENT "Rameau's Temperament"
1784 - Clementi (1752-1832) - "C-E wide, E-G# wider, A♭-C wider still"	
1786 - Barca rediscovers Vallotti's temp.	
1800 - Young (1773-1829)	
	1801 - Clementi (1752-1832)
1806 - Stanhope (1753-1816) - 1/3,	
1812 - Crotch (1775-1847)	
	1828 - Hummel (1778-1837)
1832 - Jousse	
	1833 - Crotch (1775-1847)
1840 - Schindler (1795-1864) — recalls Beethoven's interest in expressiveness of keys	

A PARALLEL CHRONOLOGY

PYTHAGOREAN TUNING	MEANTONE "Praetorius' Temperament"
1600 - present - Pythag. still in day-to-day use in provincial areas	
	1847 - meantone used as circulating (well) temperament
	1874 - Pole (1814-1900)

OF TUNING GENRES

WELL TEMPERAMENT	EQUAL TEMPERAMENT "Rameau's Temperament"
	1843 - Broadwood adopts = temp.
	1851 - Great Exhibition - organs built/rebuilt after this show = temp. specified
1970 - van Biezen rediscovers Vallotti's temperament	
1982 - Fairchild rediscovers Vallotti's temperament	

APPENDIX II

HOW TO CONSTRUCT

A TUNING RECIPE

As performers we don't have to construct our own tuning recipes, but if we want to, here's a method that involves nothing more than ordinary arithmetic and yet is accurate enough for practical use. First, we must define what type or genre of tuning we're about to deal with. If the tuning is stated in theoretical writings, this will probably be just a matter of careful reading and historically accurate interpretation of the author's language. If the tuning occurs in practical or pedagogical writing, it may be so vague as to require substantial additional research to set its parameters. Jeffrey Evans' realization of Godfrey Keller's 18th-century meantone in volume 11 of *Early Music* is a masterful demonstration of this process. In some rare cases, a practical statement of a tuning may contain enough internal information for it to be deduced accurately without much outside research. My analysis and realization of Roger North's 1726 meantone (scheduled for publication in 1989) is a good example of this process.

Part and parcel of defining the tuning is to decide what comma is going to be dealt with and how it's going to be handled. A comma is a discrepancy between two pure intervals or groups of pure intervals. This discrepancy is usually expressed in terms of a microinterval called a "cent" which was invented for theoretical purposes in the late 1800's by Alexander Ellis. One cent (1¢) is 1/100 of an equal-tempered semitone, and since it is a division of a tempered interval, an interval which does not occur in nature, it's obvious that no natural interval, including those intervals called commas, can be expressed accurately in whole numbers of cents.

The two commas most often encountered in constructing tuning recipes are the syntonic comma (also called the Ptolemaic or Didymic comma) and the ditonic (or Pythagorean) comma. The syntonic comma is the difference between two pure octaves plus one pure major third and four pure fifths stacked one on top of the other. It is usually said to be 22¢ wide (the stack of fifths is wider than the octaves and third), but a more accurate measure is 21.51¢. It must be dealt with in tunings which contain pure thirds and sometimes in tunings in which the circle of fifths is not closed (i.e., most meantone tunings). In the common meantone tuning attributed to Praetorius, it is divided into 4 parts which are then parceled out to the four fifths which must "fit inside" each pure major third — hence the term "1/4-comma."

The ditonic comma is the excess of 12 fifths, stacked one on top of the other, over 7 similarly arranged octaves, and it must be dealt with in all tunings which offer enharmonicity or which claim to have no wolf intervals. (A wolf interval, incidentally, is usually caused by not dividing a comma and merely stashing it whole in an out-of-the-way place where, in the opinion of the tuning's author, it probably won't bother anybody. Pythagorean tuning, with its famous $G^\#$-E^b wolf, is an outstanding example of this practice.) The ditonic comma is usually specified as being 24¢ wide, but again, a more accurate figure which is sometimes needed is 23.46¢.

Once we have decided which comma is being divided and where those divisions are to be placed, we're ready to proceed. To convert our theoretical tuning into a practical recipe, we have to pick a starting frequency which is appropriate to the starting note of the tuning. If middle C is used as a starting point, we may use modern day pitch (261.626 Herz) or, if we prefer, low pitch (204.468 Herz, one equal-tempered half step lower). (Any frequency can be moved up or down by equal-tempered semitones by multiplying or dividing it by the 12th root of 2, which is 1.0594631. 261.626 divided by 1.0594631 = 204.468.)

It's easiest to depart from C via a pure interval and then temper that interval afterwards if our tuning so requires. To create pure intervals from C, follow these instructions:

M3↑○ if the interval is C-E (major third up), multiply the frequency of C by 5 and then divide that number by 4;

M3↓○ if the interval is A^b-C (major third down), multiply the frequency of C by 4 and divide the result by 5;

P4↑○ if the interval is C-F (perfect fourth up), multiply C by 4 and divide the result by 3;

P4↓○ if the interval is G-C (perfect fourth down), multiply C by 3 and divide the result by 4;

P5↑○ if the interval is C-G (perfect fifth up), multiply C by 3 and divide the result by 2;

P5↓∘   if the interval is F-C (perfect fifth down), multiply C by 2 and and divide the result by 3;

m3↑∘   if the interval is C-E^b (minor third up), multiply C by 6 and divide the result by 5;

m3↓∘   if the interval is A-C (minor third down), multiply C by 5 and divide the result by 6.

There are other pure intervals we could create from C, but these will probably be sufficient for most situations.

If our first interval from C is to remain pure, we merely notate the frequency we've computed above and proceed to the next note in our tuning chain. Sometimes we might return immediately to C and go off in another direction, but usually we take the note we've just computed, use that frequency to find the frequency of another note, and so on until all 12 notes in the octave have been computed. Meantone usually requires a return to C and departure in the opposite direction sooner or later.

If our first interval is to be tempered, then the frequency of the note we computed as a pure interval from C will have to be adjusted as follows. Let "x" = 1.00057779.

    M3↑+ To widen C-E (major third up),

multiply the frequency of E by x once for each 1¢ wider than pure C-E is to be. If C-E is to be 4¢ wider than pure, multiply the frequency of E four successive times by x.

M3↑− To narrow C-E (major third up), divide the frequency of E by x once for each cent the interval is to be narrowed.

M3↓+ To widen A^b-C (major third down), divide the frequency of A^b by x once for each cent the interval is to be widened.

M3↓− To narrow A^b-C (major third down), multiply the frequency of A^b by x once for each cent the interval is to be narrowed.

P4↑+ To widen C-F (perfect fourth up) multiply the frequency of F by x once for each cent the interval is to be widened.

P4↑− To narrow C-F (perfect fourth up), divide the frequency of F by x once for each cent the interval is to be narrowed.

P4↓+ To widen G-C (perfect fourth down), divide the frequency of G by x once for each cent the interval is to be widened.

P4↓− To narrow G-C (perfect fourth down), multiply the frequency of G by x once for each cent the interval is to be narrowed.

P5↑+ To widen C-G (perfect fifth up), multiply the frequency of G by x once for each cent the interval is to be widened.

P5↑− To narrow C-G (perfect fifth up), divide the frequency of G by x once for each cent the interval is to be narrowed.

P5↓+ To widen F-C (perfect fifth down), divide the frequency of F by x once for each cent the interval is to be widened.

P5↓− To narrow F-C (perfect fifth down), multiply the frequency of F by x once for each cent the interval is to be narrowed.

m3↑+ To widen C-E^b (minor third up), multiply the frequency of E^b by x once for each cent the interval is to be widened.

m3↑− To narrow C-E^b (minor third up) divide the frequency of E^b by x once for each cent the interval is to be narrowed.

m3↓+ To widen A-C (minor third down), divide the frequency of A by x once for each cent the interval is to be widened.

m3↓- To narrow A-C (minor third down), multiply the frequency of A by x once for each cent the interval is to be narrowed.

This may seem like tedious, computer writing on a first reading, but it's nice later not to have to reread the whole section if we just have one simple question while constructing a tuning recipe. Incidentally, our "x" factor, 1.00057779, is just the 1200th root of 2, or the numerical equivalent of Ellis' cent.

Following this procedure of creating pure intervals and tempering them by various numbers of cents as needed yields a list of 12 frequencies, one for each note. These 12 frequencies may not all be in the same octave, so we can fill in gaps in our list by either multiplying a frequency by 2 to get the frequency of the note an octave higher, or dividing by 2 to get the frequency of the note an octave lower.

Now, with our table of frequencies, we're ready to create a table of beat rates for various intervals that we can use in tuning. This will be easiest to notate if we use staff paper, allocating one line for each type interval. On the first line we might notate all the major thirds in this temperament chromatically, beginning with C-E and ending with B-D#. On the next line we could put fourths, and then further down, fifths and minor thirds. (Remembering the equal-beating characteristics of our P4-P5 and m3-M6 octave checks, we could save time and space by stacking fifths on top of fourths on one line, and stacking major sixths on their contiguous minor thirds on another.) Over each interval we write the beats per second we calculate will be created when we play it, along with a corresponding metronome marking (beats per second x 60). Here's how to calculate beats:

    M3   For C-E, multiply the C by 5 and the E by 4 and figure the difference. If C x 5 is greater than E x 4, the third is narrow; if E x 4 is greater than C x 5, the third is wide.

    P4   For C-F, multiply C by 4 and F by 3 and figure the difference. If C x 4 is greater than F x 3, the fourth is narrow; if F x 3 is greater than C x 4, the fourth is wide.

    P5   For C-G, multiply C by 3 and G by 2 and figure the difference. If C x 3 is greater than G x 2, the fifth is narrow; if G x 2 is greater than C x 3, the fifth is wide.

m3 For C-E^b, multiply C by 6 and E^b by 5 and figure the difference. If C x 6 is greater than E^b x 5, the minor third is narrow; if E^b x 5 is greater than C x 6, the minor third is wide.

Once our table of beat speeds is complete, we're in a position to see whether there are any equal-beating intervals which might be used in tuning. Remember, however, that if two intervals which are equal-beating share a central note, they must both be wide or both be narrow for their equal-beating quality to be useful in tuning. For instance, in most temperaments we could observe that the A-D fourth and its contiguous D-A fifth both share a note in common and beat the same. The fact that they beat the same is useless for tempering purposes, however, because if the octave A-A stays pure, they will continue to beat the same wherever the D is set. Since A-D is usually wide and D-A is usually narrow, manipulation of D is only useful in tuning if we count beats while setting it.

And that's it as far as generation of raw information goes. If the tuning we're constructing came with a specified line or group of intervals to be used, we simply insert our beat speeds and metronome markings above those intervals and follow them. If the tuning's author didn't suggest a tempering pattern, or if we see another pattern which will achieve the same result with superior accuracy or ease, we proceed to notate whatever scheme or recipe we think will work best. Nothing substitutes well for experience in this phase of creating a tuning recipe, so the sooner we begin trying, the sooner our skills will increase.

CRITICAL BIBLIOGRAPHY
(Note: see Appendix I for explanation of abbreviations below)

Barbour, J. Murray. "Bach and the Art of Temperament," *Musical Quarterly*, XXXIII (January, 1947), 64-89. Examines also works/preferences of Kuhnau, Couperin, Telemann, Purcell (cf. Meffen) and Rameau. 13 temperaments given in cents.

────────── *History of Unequal Temperaments.* Recordings and liner notes. Jackson Heights, NY: Misurgia Records, 1958(?).

────────── "Irregular Systems of Temperament," *Journal of the American Musicological Society*, I (Fall, 1948), 20–26. Temperaments by historical writers and by the author with mean deviation and standard deviation computations to show how much they differ from equal temperament.

────────── and Fritz A. Kuttner. *Meantone Temperament in Theory and Practice.* Recordings and liner notes. Jackson Heights, NY:

Misurgia Records, 1958. Lots of math. Much info out of date. 1/4, examples from Tallis, Merula, Gibbons, Trabachi, Rossi, Couperin, Zipoli, Handel, and Bach; 1/6, examples all Bach (incl. 4 from WTC!).

——————— *Tuning and Temperament.* New York: Da Capo, 1972. The classic examination of a multitude of temperaments vis-à-vis equal temperament.

Barnes, John. "Bach's Keyboard Temperament: Internal Evidence from the Well-Tempered Clavier," *Early Music* VII (April, 1979), 236-249. Intervals in the "48" subjected to statistical evaluation heavily dependent on subjective judgment of "prominence." Result: Vallotti with the last tempered fifth pushed up to B-F# (E-B pure). See also related letters in *Early Music* VIII (October, 1980), 511-513.

Billeter, Bernhard. "Anweisung zum Stimmen von Tasteninstrumenten in Verschiedenen Temperaturen," *Österreichische Musikzeitschrift* XXXII (April, 1977), 185-195. Some math. Elementary discussion of and tuning directions for equal temperament, meantone with variable thirds, Schlick,

Werckmeister, Silbermann, and a WTC tuning derived from Silbermann.

——————— "Die Silbermann-Stimmungen," *Archiv für Musikwissenschaft* XXVII (1970), 73-85. Five interpretations of 1/6, meantone (incl. one by the author) compared with each other and with three related temperaments.

Blood, William." 'Well-Tempering' the Clavier: Five Methods," *Early Music* VII (October, 1979), 491-495. Tuning recipes for Werckmeister, Vallotti, and 3 Neidhardt temperaments.

Bodky, Erwin. *The Interpretation of Bach's Keyboard Works.* Cambridge: Harvard University Press, 1960. pp. 229-230: "It would be worthless to tabulate Bach's works for the purpose of finding out whether generalizations about the use of keys can be made. Since he transposed not only single pieces (e.g., the Fugue in A flat major, W.K. II, was originally written in F major) but also whole works when he wanted to have a certain scheme of keys complete (the French Overture, originally written in C minor, was transposed to B minor so that this key could be represented in the *Klavierübung*), he could not have considered the choice of a key of any significance in regard to establishing a given mood."

Curtis, Alan. *Sweelinck's Keyboard Music.* Leiden: Leiden University Press, 1972. pp. 143-147: quotes Barbour, calls Werckmeister "a man . . . continually identified with equal temperament," and suggests that *wohl temperiert* refers to a modified meantone system.

Evans, Jeffrey. "The keyboard tuning rules of *The Modern Musick-master,*" *Early Music* XI (July, 1983), 360-363. Deduces that Keller's instructions require P5– 3-4$^{1}/2$¢ and M3+ 4–10¢.

Farey, John. "On Music," *The Philosophical Magazine* XXVI (1807), 171-176. 1/5, irregular temperament.

Jorgensen, Owen. *Tuning the Historical Temperaments by Ear.* Marquette: Northern Michigan University Press, 1977. 89 recipes for 51 tunings and temperaments.

Kellner, Herbert Anton. "A Mathematical Approach Reconstituting J. S.

Bach's Keyboard Temperament," *Bach* X (1979), 2-9.

——— "Das Wohltemperierte Clavier: Tuning and Musical Structure," *English Harpsichord Magazine* II (April, 1980), 137-140.

Klop, G. C. *Harpsichord Tuning*, trans. Glen Wilson. Garderen: Werkplaats voor Clavecimbelbouw, 1974. Nice intro to subject. Some math. 14 temperaments. Vallotti attributed to van Biezen.

Kuhnle, Wesley. *History of Tuning Practice, 15th to 20th Centuries.* Los Angeles, 1959. (Unpublished tape recordings and notes in possession of Paul Kuhnle.) Tunings explained through interesting if sometimes inappropriate examples. Acoustic rather than historical approach to tuning selection.

——— *Tune it Yourself. Why?* Los Angeles, 1962. (Unpublished tuning manual in possession of M. Tittle.) Contains 3 just intonation schemes; the Ramos transposition of Pythagorean; 1/4, 1/6, and an odd Marpurg meantone; equal temperament; and 2 temperaments by the author: a well temperament and a tempered Pythagorean (the latter suggested for English virginal music on acoustic grounds.)

Lecky, James. "Temperaments," *A Dictionary of Music and Musicians*, ed. Sir George Grove, D.C.L. London: Macmillan, 1893.

Lindley, Mark. "Early 16th-Century Keyboard Temperaments," *Musica Disciplina* XXVIII (1974), 129-151. Schlick, Aron, Lanfranco: original text cited with line-by-line parallel translation.

———— "Equal Temperament," "Just Intonation," "Meantone," "Pythagorean Intonation," "Temperaments," "Well-Tempered Clavier," *The New Grove Dictionary of Music and Musicians*, ed. Stanley Sadie. London: Macmillan, 1980. "Must" reading.

———— "Fifteenth-Century Evidence for Meantone Temperament," *Proceedings of the Royal Musical Association* CII (1975-76), 37-51. Ramos, Spataro, Gaffurius texts explored as above.

———— "Instructions for the Clavier Diversely Tempered," *Early Music* V (January, 1977), 18-23. Tuning schemes for Pythagorean (original $G^{\#}$-E^b and B-G^b

transposition); 1/4, meantone; equal temperament; *tempérament ordinaire;* Werckmeister; and Vallotti.

————— "Mersenne on Keyboard Tuning," *Journal of Music Theory* XXIV (Fall, 1980), 167-195. Discusses just, meantone, and equal temperament with line-by-line translations as above.

Link, John W., Jr. *The Mathematics of Music.* 1967. (Unpublished manuscript in possession of M. Tittle.) Little text; lots of tables and numbers.

————— "The Promise of Meantone," *Diapason* LIX (January, 1968), 22-24. Meantone explained with profuse mathematics.

Lloyd, Llewellyn S. "Temperaments," *Grove's Dictionary of Music and Musicians*, ed. Eric Blom. London: Macmillan, 1954.

McClain, Ernest G. "Pythagorean Paper Folding: A Study in Tuning and Temperament," *Mathematics Teacher* LXIII (March, 1970), 233-237. Spatial demonstration of the mathematical properties of various tuning systems.

McClure, A. R. "Studies in Keyboard Temperaments," *Galpin Society Journal* I (1948), 28-40. Discussion of the 19-note octave (1/3, meantone) and the Robt. Smith 5/18, meantone.

McGeary, Thomas. "Early Eighteenth-Century English Harpsichord Tuning and Stringing," *English Harpsichord Magazine* III (April, 1982), 18-22. Reports 1/4, meantone modified à la Mersenne from 1730.

Mackenzie of Ord, Alexander C. N. *Keyboard Temperament in England during the Eighteenth and Nineteenth Centuries.* University of Bristol, 1983. (Unpublished dissertation.)

Meffen, John. *A Harpsichord Tuning Manual.* Darlington, 1978. (Unpublished manuscript in possession of M. Tittle.) Well-documented. 15 temperaments described in cents with tuning recipes.

———— "A Question of Temperament: Purcell and Croft," *Musical Times* CXIX (June, 1978), 504-506. Suggests regular meantone for Purcell and *tempérament ordinaire* for Croft.

———— *The Temperament of Keyboard Instruments in England during the Late Sixteenth and Early Seventeenth Centuries.* Durham University, 1973. (Unpublished Master's Thesis.) Extensive examination of tunings as revealed through music literature. 1/4, meantone with occasional dissonances the norm; the Bull *Fantasia* intended for the clavicymbalum universale.

———— *The Temperament of Keyboard Instruments in England from the Virginalists to the middle of the Nineteenth Century.* University of Leeds, 1977. (Unpublished dissertation.) Suggests meantone (1/5,?) up to the time of Croft in the early 1700's, then *tempérament ordinaire* to mid-century (Handel excepted), then Werckmeister and Vallotti joined at century-end by equal temperament.

Pollard, Victor. *Tuning and Temperament in Southern Germany to the End of the Seventeenth Century.* University of Leeds, 1985. (Unpublished dissertation.) Elegant new translations of Agricola, Schlick, Praetorius, and Werckmeister.

Rayner, Clare G. "The Enigmatic Cima: Meantone Tuning and Transpositions," *Galpin Society Journal* XX (1969), 23-34.

Sargent, George. "Eighteenth-century Tuning Directions: Precise Intervallic Determination," *The Music Review* XXX (February, 1969), 27-34. Treats North, Türk, the Avison MS., and others.

Stanhope, Charles Earl. "Principles of the Science of Tuning Instruments with Fixed Tones," *The Philosophical Magazine* XXV (1806), 291-312. Recommends a 1/3, well temperament with complications. "When I began this inquiry I had the curiosity to converse with 16 or 18 of the most eminent musicians in England upon this subject. Half of them did then approve of what is called THE EQUAL TEMPERAMENT . . . . The other half, on the contrary, reprobated that mode of tuning . . . "

Thomas, Michael. "The Tunings and Pitch of Early Clavichords," *English Harpsichord Magazine* I (April, 1976), 175-180. Discusses the clavichord of Arnaut de Zwolle and the Intarsia at Urbino.

Tittle, Martin B. *The Roger North Keyboard Tuning of 1726: Analysis and Reconstruction.* Ann Arbor: Anderson Press, (sched. 1989).

van Biezen, J. *Stemmingen, Speciaal bij Toetsinstrumenten.* Stichting: Centrum voor de Kerkzang, n.d. A handbook: some math; discussion of Pythagorean; 1/4, and 1/6, meantone; Werckmeister; Vallotti; and others.

Williams, Peter. "Equal Temperament and the English Organ, 1675-1825," *Acta Musicologica* XL (January-March, 1968), 53-65.